THE GOOD NEWS GOES VIRAL

by
Gwynne Watkins

Beat by Beat Press
www.bbbpress.com

All rights reserved. No part of this book may be reproduced or transmitted in any form or by any means, electronic or mechanical, including photocopying, recording or any other storage and retrieval system, without the written permission of the author or publisher.

For any form of non-amateur presentation, including but not limited to professional theater, stage, television and radio permission must be obtained from the author or publisher.

Published by Beat by Beat Press
www.bbbpress.com

Copyright © 2021 by Gwynne Watkins

THE GOOD NEWS GOES VIRAL

OVERVIEW

Every scene in this Christmas play is a separate "video message" between Biblical characters.

Title Cards should be shown at the beginning of each scene. If you do not wish to use Title Cards, you may choose to read them as narration. The play can also be performed without them, though we believe they add some clarity to the story.

The settings described in each video call are meant to spark your imagination. Use whatever you have at home to create the scene and costumes! There are opportunities here to incorporate siblings, pets, and Christmas decorations – but it's fine to keep things simple, too!

This play can be performed as a series of socially-distanced monologues if in-person performance is an option.

Finally, while the playwright has taken liberties with the text, all characters and events are adapted from the Christmas story as it appears in Matthew 1:18-2:1-12 and Luke 1:26-56, 2:1-21.

CHARACTERS

Angel 1 (Gabriel)

Elizabeth, Mary's cousin

Joseph, Mary's fiancé

Angel 2

Emperor Caesar Augustus

Donkey

Innkeeper

Angel Choir (1 or more actors)

Magi (1 or more actors)

Shepherds (1 or more actors, plus optional sheep)

Mary, Jesus' mother

Character Notes:

Scenes with one or more actors are intended for siblings or people in the same household.

If working with a smaller cast, the same Angel can perform all three Angel scenes.

THE GOOD NEWS
GOES VIRAL

THE GOOD NEWS GOES VIRAL

By Gwynne Watkins

♫ *OPENING SONG: "O Come, All Ye Faithful" (Optional)* ♫

TITLE CARD #1 (INTRODUCTION)

[NOTE: These Title Cards may also be read as narration.]

The Christmas story is all about delivering God's message of Good News: A Savior is born!

Everyone from Mary to the angels to the shepherds plays a role in sharing God's news.

But what if, during the very first Christmas, everyone had to communicate using phones and computers like we do now?

Here is the story of the first Christmas, as told through a series of video messages.

First up: Mary is getting an unexpected call from Heaven...

In ancient Israel, in the small town of Nazareth, lives a young woman named Mary, who is pledged to be married to a man named Joseph.

One otherwise ordinary day, she receives a call from an angel named Gabriel.

SCENE #1: ANGEL 1

(Scene: ANGEL 1 calls Mary from Heaven.)

(Light everywhere. Glitter. Feathers. Stars. Fluffy clouds. Harps. You know, Heaven.)

(The Angel has two props. The first is a piece of paper rolled up like a scroll, which is THE MESSAGE. The second is a CELEBRATION OBJECT: a handful of confetti, a horn to blow, something that says "Yay!")

(ANGEL 1 speaks directly to the camera.)

ANGEL 1

Hi Mary!

Sorry to show up out of nowhere like this, but I have a very important message for you and it just can't wait.

Oh, I'm Gabriel, by the way. Angel. Hi.

So here it is:

(Gabriel unrolls The Message and reads to Mary:)

Mary, you have been chosen by God.

You are going to have a baby.

Your baby will be the son of God!

(Gabriel throws the message away and uses the Celebration Object.)

Congratulations!

So you may be asking, how is this possible?

Well -- you know how your cousin Elizabeth was too old to have a baby, but now she's six months pregnant?

That's because nothing is impossible with God!
Your son will be called Wonderful Counselor, Mighty God, Prince of Peace --

but you should call him Jesus, which means "God saves."

Congratulations, Mary! And Hallelujah!

> *(Gabriel uses the Celebration Object again and parties as the call ends.)*

TITLE CARD #2

Mary's cousin Elizabeth lives out in the country with her husband Zechariah, a priest.

Like the angel said, Elizabeth is expecting a baby. Her son will be one day be called John the Baptist.

When she learns of Mary's news, Elizabeth calls her cousin to celebrate.

SCENE #2: ELIZABETH

(Scene: ELIZABETH, Mary's older cousin, calls Mary.)

(Elizabeth is at home in the country. She is 6 months pregnant.)

(Maybe we see remnants of a recent baby shower: blue balloons, gifts, "It's a boy!" signs.)

(Objects around her may include a picture of a sonogram, prenatal vitamins, a book of baby names.)

(When she calls, she might be eating pickles or ice cream.)

(ELIZABETH speaks directly to the camera.)

ELIZABETH

Mary! I just your message! I can't believe it! Aaaaa!

I CAN believe it, though. Because an angel visited us too.

When the angel said I was going to have a baby after all these years? I actually laughed.

But it was true.

And when I learned you were pregnant, I felt my baby jump inside me! And I knew: your baby is really the son of God.

> *(Singing, maybe to the tune of "The Venga Bus is Coming")*

The son of God's your baby, the son of God's your baby...

So excited. Our boys will be cousins!

What are you thinking for names? I call dibs on John.

Oh. And what are you going to tell Joseph?

TITLE CARD #3

Joseph, Mary's fiance, also lives in Nazareth, where he works as a carpenter.

When Mary tells him her news, he is excited but worried.

Joseph calls Mary from work.

SCENE #3: JOSEPH

(Scene: JOSEPH, Mary's fiancé, calls Mary.)

(Joseph is at work. He is a carpenter. He sits in his workshop, or perhaps on the outskirts of a construction site. If siblings are present, they could be working in the background.)

(He might wear a hardhat, goggles, an apron, or other protective gear. He is surrounded by tools. Maybe he is hammering a nail into a board or sanding a surface.)

(JOSEPH speaks directly to the camera.)

JOSEPH

Hi Mary,

I've been thinking about what you've said – that you're having God's baby.

This is unexpected.

I just have a few questions.

Like, will the baby call me "Dad," or "Other Dad?"

Also: I've never been a Dad. How will I know what to do?

(Beginning to panic:)

Usually when I don't know how to do something, I read the instruction manual.

But there is no instruction manual.

(Full-on panicking:)

HOW AM I SUPPOSED TO RAISE GOD'S BABY WITHOUT AN INSTRUCTION MANUAL?

(Joseph takes a deep breath.)

I'm sorry, Mary. I don't want to freak out.
I just wish an angel had visited me too. Maybe then I wouldn't be so nervous.

But hey -- if we can't have an instruction manual, I'm glad we have each other.

Guess I should start building a crib?

TITLE CARD #4

That same night, God sends an angel to visit Joseph in a dream.

The angel calls Joseph to reassure him.

SCENE #4: ANGEL 2

(Scene: ANGEL 2 calls Joseph from Heaven.)

(It may be a different neighborhood, but the description from Call #1 applies: glitter, lights, etc.)

(Angel 2 is a little flustered -- they meant to make this call earlier!)

(Because Joseph is skeptical, Angel 2 will need to offer ANGEL PROOF: a quick, effective action to demonstrate that they are actually an angel. Such as: They clap and a bright light shines on them; they sing a heavenly note; they play a chord on the harp; they summon a "Hallelujah!" from Handel's Hallelujah Chorus; they put on a halo or point to their wings. They will do this when indicated in the script.)

(ANGEL 2 speaks directly to the camera.)

ANGEL 2

Joseph! Hi!

Sorry for the delay. Lots going on here. Heaven is preparing for the birth of a Savior -- it's a big deal!

Anyway. Didn't mean to leave you hanging.

As you can see, I'm an angel.

(Angel 2 does their ANGEL PROOF.)

And I know you're afraid. But you should not be.

Because Mary's baby is the child of the Holy Spirit.

Mary has been chosen by God, and you have been chosen by Mary.

Together you will raise the Messiah, who will be the savior of all people.

Hope that clears things up.

Oh -- and his name is Jesus.

Bye!

> *(Maybe they do the ANGEL PROOF one last time before they go, but that's the end of the call.)*

TITLE CARD #5

In Mary's final month of pregnancy, Emperor Caesar Augustus issues a decree to the whole Roman Empire that a census will be taken. All citizens, including Mary and Joseph, must travel to their home towns to be registered.

The Emperor sends this message to all the people.

SCENE #5: EMPEROR CAESAR AUGUSTUS

(Scene: EMPEROR CAESAR AUGUSTUS announces that all citizens of the Roman Empire must return to their hometowns for the census.)

(AUGUSTUS was the first Roman Emperor. He should be played by a very small, very loud child, in a toga if possible.)

(AUGUSTUS speaks directly to the camera.)

EMPEROR CAESAR AUGUSTUS
I am Caesar!
Go home!

(End of call.)

TITLE CARD #6

Joseph and Mary are descendants of King David, so they must travel a long ways to Bethlehem, which is the City of David.

Since they are peasants, they do not bring much on the journey: just some food and water, and a donkey to carry them.

After walking for miles across the desert, that donkey has a word for Joseph.

SCENE #6: DONKEY

(Scene: DONKEY, a donkey, calls Joseph.)

(Donkey is traveling with Joseph, so the call should come from outside, or someplace that looks like a desert. Maybe there's a tent. We might see stars.)

(Donkey should have something to carry, maybe a backpack or a giant pile of snacks.)

(DONKEY speaks directly to the camera.)

DONKEY

Hey Joseph, it's me, your donkey.

The one who's been carrying your stuff for SEVENTY MILES?

Look, I get it. I'm a donkey. I carry stuff. I'm good at it. See?

(Donkey demonstrates.)

But Bethlehem, your hometown, is really far from Nazareth! I've never walked so much in my life.

Plus Mary is like nine months pregnant -- shouldn't she be home resting or something?

Then again, what do I know? I'm just a donkey.

(Donkey pauses to think for a moment.)

You and Mary talk a lot about God. Maybe God is watching over me too. And if so, maybe God could find me a nice, warm stable to rest in when we get to Bethlehem.

Here's hoping!

TITLE CARD #7

Mary and Joseph arrive in Bethlehem. Unfortunately, they have trouble finding a place to stay.

Though the inn is full, the innkeeper calls Mary and Joseph with a suggestion for where they can spend the night.

SCENE #7: INNKEEPER

(Scene: THE INNKEEPER speaks to Mary and Joseph.)

(Obviously the Innkeeper is at the inn. They could be at the front desk with a reservation book and a bell. Or they're standing at the front door, which has a sign that says "Bethlehem Inn." They could even be standing by the stable.)

(The Innkeeper should have an animal, a pet or toy, to hold up during the scene. If no animal is available, the line "All of our animals are very friendly. See?" can be cut.)

(INNKEEPER speaks directly to the camera.)

INNKEEPER

Hi Mary and Joseph,

Welcome to the Bethlehem Inn!

So I have good news and bad news and good news.

The good news is, business is booming! The census has got us totally booked up through the end of the year. We can finally build that pool!

The bad news is, we don't have a room for you at this time.

The good news is, we have this lovely stable, plenty of space to spread out, lots of free hay. Just push the cows aside and I think you'll be very comfortable.

All of our animals are very friendly. See?

(The Innkeeper holds up an animal.)

Plus, I'll give you an excellent rate.

You're not expecting any visitors are you?

TITLE CARD #8

That night, Mary gives birth to baby Jesus in a stable in Bethlehem.

At that very same moment, a group of shepherds is watching their sheep in a field outside the city. Suddenly, a choir of angels appears to them in the sky... with a message.

SCENE #8: ANGEL CHOIR

(Scene: THE ANGEL CHOIR calls the Shepherds.)

(The angels in this scene can be played by any number of siblings, or a combination of parents and children. Divide up the lines however it makes sense. Repeated lines in parentheses are optional if you have more than one actor in the scene.)

(The Angel Choir can be in their own corner of Heaven, or against a simple night sky.)

(THE ANGELS speak directly to the camera.)

ANGEL CHOIR

Hello shepherds!

Do not be afraid!

We have been sent from Heaven to deliver Good News!
(Good News!)

Today a Savior has been born!

He will be like a good shepherd, caring for all people.

He will bring light and hope to the world.

Glory to God in the highest!
(Glory to God in the Highest!)

Peace on Earth!
(Peace on Earth!)

You will find the baby in Bethlehem, lying in a manger.

What are you waiting for? Go!
(Go! Go!)

TITLE CARD #9

Meanwhile, The Magi have travelled from the East, following a new star that appeared in the sky. These scholars and scientists know the prophecy of Jesus' birth and seek the baby who will be called the Messiah.

The Magi have been instructed to report to King Herod in Jerusalem when they find the baby. But an angel has told them not to trust King Herod, so the Magi send him this message.

SCENE #9: MAGI

(Scene: THE MAGI report to King Herod.)

(The Magi (or Wise Men) don't need to be men, and there don't need to be three of them. Any number will do. If there are multiple speakers, divide up these lines however it makes sense.)

(The Magi should look very fancy. Pile on the jewelry.)

(If possible, we should see The Star in the background.)

(They have a MAP, and three GIFTS represented by household objects.)

(THE MAGI speak directly to the camera.)

MAGI

Hi Herod,

Magi here with a quick update.

We have been following this star for seven days now, and it looks like it has settled over a little town in Judea.

(The Magi consult a map.)

So that's where we're headed!

And we picked up a few gifts for the Messiah. We have:

gold,
frankincense,
and myrrh.

(The Magi hold up household objects to represent the gifts.)

We thought about getting something more practical, like diapers, but we think these gifts really say:

You're the most special baby who has ever been born.

So we're going to continue our journey.

(The Magi speak this line very quickly;)

And then we're going to go home a different way, because God told us in a dream that you're evil and we shouldn't go back there. Bye!

TITLE CARD #10

Back in Bethlehem, the shepherds have followed the angels' directions and found the baby Jesus. They are joyful and amazed! They send this message to share the Good News with the whole world.

SCENE #10: SHEPHERDS

(Scene: THE SHEPHERDS deliver the Good News.)

(This scene is for at least one SHEPHERD and one SHEEP, but the more the merrier.)

(Divide the shepherds' lines among actors in whatever way makes sense.)

(If there are no actors to play sheep, the sheep can be represented by a toy, a puppet, a picture, or even someone off camera making sheep noises.)

(The Shepherds are calling from outside the Stable where Jesus has been born. The stable can be a nativity set, an improvised creche with a doll or baby sibling, or a picture.)

(THE SHEPHERDS speak directly to the camera.)

SHEPHERDS

This is a message for all the people in the world.

We are shepherds, and we don't get out a lot.

Jesse here hasn't taken a bath in a year!

It's true.

Mostly we live out in the fields and take care of our sheep. You probably don't think about us much.

But tonight! Something amazing happened.

God sent angels to tell us -

Us!

- that a Savior had been born in Bethlehem.

They said, look for the baby lying in a manger. A manger. Like the thing cows eat from.

So we said, where do you find cows in a city? And we thought - in a stable.

And sure enough, here's a stable with a giant star over it.

And look - there's the baby.

(The Shepherds turn the camera to Baby Jesus.)

They call him Jesus.

That cute little baby is the Messiah who will save everyone in the world, even nobodies like us.

But you know what? God chose us to tell the world about Jesus. So we're not nobodies.

And whoever you are, you're not a nobody either, because this baby was born to save you too.

SHEEP
Baa! Baa!

SHEPHERDS
We gotta get back to our sheep!

Spread the good news, Jesus is born!

TITLE CARD #11

This has been an extraordinary time for Mary, and now that she is a mother, a new adventure begins.

Mary has been treasuring all of these strange and wonderful events in her heart. When she finally gets a quiet moment, Mary shares a message with Jesus.

SCENE #11: MARY

(Scene: MARY has a heart-to-heart with Jesus.)

(Mary speaks into the camera, so she doesn't necessarily need to be holding a baby. But she could.)

(She is in the stable or at home. The setting should be warm, cozy, magical. Maybe a Christmas tree or a fireplace in the background.)

(MARY speaks directly to the camera.)

MARY

Hi Jesus. I'm your mom.

It's so nice to finally meet you.

The world has been waiting a long time for you. I've only been waiting nine months but it felt like forever.

You are going to change our lives.

Your story will be told over and over again. And it starts right here.

So this is what I want you to know:

The day you were born, you were surrounded by love.

God's love shone through you like a light, and people came from all over, just to feel it.

I'd watch them come into the stable, cautious and weary. Then they'd see you. And suddenly, they would be full of hope.

I have a feeling you'll never stop surprising me. People might be scared or confused by you, but if they let you in, they'll feel it. The hope. The love.

You are the light of the world, and I am proud to be your mother.

Happy birthday, my son.

♪ **_CLOSING SONG: "Joy to the World" (Optional)_** ♪

THE END.

Optional Music

It is up to you whether to include music with this production. If interested, a simple option is to download the **Beat by Beat Christmas Singles Collection** - instrumental versions of 10 traditional hymns arranged for kids to sing. You may use these tracks in any way that makes sense for your production - either as underscoring to the title cards, underscoring to the scenes, or as performance opportunities for your congregation. We have indicated a few suggested placements throughout the script.

You can listen to samples of the **Christmas Singles Collection** and instantly purchase for download at:

https://www.bbbpress.com/songs-for-kids

Below is a list of the songs included in the **Beat by Beat Christmas Singles Collection**:

O Come, All Ye Faithful

Away in a Manger

Hark! The Herald Angels Sing

We Three Kings

Joy to the World

Jingle Bells

Go Tell it on the Mountain

O Holy Night

The First Noel

Silent Night

ABOUT THE AUTHOR

GWYNNE WATKINS is a playwright and lyricist. Her work for children includes the musicals *Tea with Chachaji* (Making Books Sing, NYC) and *Space Pirates!* (Garden Players, Forest Hills NY), the three-play series *In Between Worlds* (New Players, Ridgewood NJ), and the nativity plays *Wow!, The Mysterious Animal* and *The Mixed-Up Christmas Pageant.* Gwynne is an alumnus of the BMI Lehman Engel Musical Theatre Workshop and a member of the Dramatists Guild. A professional journalist, she lives in New York's Hudson Valley with her husband and son.

ABOUT BEAT BY BEAT PRESS

Beat by Beat Press is the world's fastest growing publisher of original, high-quality musicals for kids, songs for kids and teaching drama resources. The materials are created by a team of professional playwrights and arts educators in New York City and Los Angeles. Since launching in 2011, Beat by Beat shows have been licensed in over 75 countries around the globe.

For more information and over 120 free drama games for kids, visit us at www.bbbpress.com.

www.ingramcontent.com/pod-product-compliance
Lightning Source LLC
LaVergne TN
LVHW051210080426
835512LV00019B/3196